COUNTRY

Vol. 50, No. 4

Publisher, Patricia A. Pingry
Associate Editor, Tim Hamling
Art Director, Patrick McRae
Contributing Editors, Lansing Christman, Deana Deck, Russ Flint, Pamela Kennedy, Heidi King, Nancy Skarmeas
Editorial Asst., Donna Sigalos Budjenska

ISBN 0-8249-1109-1

IDEALS—Vol. 50, No. 4 June MCMXCIII IDEALS (ISSN 0019-137X) is published eight times a year: February, March, May, June, August, September, November, December by IDEALS PUBLISHING CORPORATION, P.O. Box 148000, Nashville, Tenn. 37214. Second-class postage paid at Nashville, Tennessee and additional mailing offices. Copyright © MCMXCIII by IDEALS PUBLISHING CORPORATION. POSTMASTER: Send address changes to Ideals, Post Office Box 148000, Nashville, Tenn. 37214-8000. All rights reserved. Title IDEALS registered U.S. Patent Office.

SINGLE ISSUE—$4.95
ONE-YEAR SUBSCRIPTION—eight consecutive issues as published—$19.95
TWO-YEAR SUBSCRIPTION—sixteen consecutive issues as published—$35.95
Outside U.S.A., add $6.00 per subscription year for postage and handling.

The cover and entire contents of IDEALS are fully protected by copyright and must not be reproduced in any manner whatsoever. Printed and bound in U.S.A.

ACKNOWLEDGMENTS

BECAUSE MEN PLOW excerpted from SONGS OF FAITH by Grace Noll Crowell. Copyright © 1939 by Grace Noll Crowell. Reprinted by arrangement with Harper San Francisco, a division of HarperCollins Publishers Inc. WHY FATHERS BOAST by Edgar A. Guest from THE LIGHT OF FAITH, copyright ©1926 by The Reilly and Lee Co. Used by permission of the author's estate. THINGS WITH A COUNTRY FLAVOR from THE GOLDEN ROAD by Edna Jaques, copyright © in Canada by Thomas Allen & Son Limited. THANKSGIVING—ON A SUMMER'S DAY from the book THE PRAYERS OF PETER MARSHALL, compiled and edited by Catherine Marshall, copyright © 1949, 1950, 1951, 1954, by Catherine Marshall. Renewed 1982. Published by Chosen Books, Fleming H. Revell—a division of Baker Book House. Our Sincere Thanks to the following authors whom we were unable to contact: Bertha Boles for COUNTRY MAGIC; Reginald Holmes for PRAYER FOR A NEW FATHER; Brian King for COUNTRY CHURCH; and Hugh M. Pierce for I HAVE A BOY.

Four-color separations by Rayson Films, Inc., Waukesha, Wisconsin.

Printing by The Banta Company, Menasha, Wisconsin.

The paper used in this publication meets the minimum requirements of American National Standard for Information Sciences—Permanence of Paper for Printed Library Materials, ANSI Z39.48-1984.

Unsolicited manuscripts will not be returned without a self-addressed stamped envelope.

Inside Front Cover
Donald Mills

Inside Back Cover
George Hinke

Cover Photo
Ed Cooper Photography

22	50 YEARS AGO
30	HANDMADE HEIRLOOM
36	A SLICE OF LIFE
42	FOR THE CHILDREN
44	READERS' REFLECTIONS
46	FROM MY GARDEN JOURNAL
48	IDEALS' FAMILY RECIPES
52	THROUGH MY WINDOW
54	COLLECTOR'S CORNER
64	BITS & PIECES
68	LEGENDARY AMERICANS
70	TRAVELER'S DIARY
74	COUNTRY CHRONICLE

BECAUSE MEN PLOW

Grace Noll Crowell

So many furrows in so many lands,
So many plows beneath men's guiding hands,
And lo! the old earth's surface has been tilled.
To meet the world's need, granaries are filled
With corn and wheat and rye from countless fields.

Because men plow, there are these golden yields;
Because their silver shares have pierced the sod
And they have worked together with their God,
The hungry world has food enough to eat
If we share wisely—and shared loaves are sweet.

The plows go down the land, the furrows run
Forever curved and deep beneath the sun:
The ancient furrows, and the fresh-turned furrows now—
There will be bread while men have faith to plow.
We thank Thee, God, for the heartening thought of men
Sowing and plowing and reaping, to plant again.

Out in the Fields

Elizabeth Barrett Browning

The little cares that fretted me,
I lost them yesterday,
Among the fields, above the sea,
Among the winds at play;
Among the lowing of the herds,
The rustling of the trees;
Among the singing of the birds,
The humming of the bees.

The foolish fears of what may happen,
I cast them all away,
Among the clover-scented grass,
Among the new-mown hay;
Among the rustling of the corn
Where drowsy poppies nod,
Where ill thoughts die and good are born—
Out in the fields with God.

BOUNTIFUL ACRES
Bunker Hill, Ohio
Fred Sieb Photography

COUNTRY MAGIC

Bertha Boles

I must be country-born at heart
Because I love all country things:
The smell of earth, fresh-wet with rain,
The sudden whir of feathered wings,

The mellow tones of hidden birds singing,
The airborne fragrance of freshly mown hay,
A killdee wheeling and plaintively crying
In the tranquil peace of fading day.

Though I may walk with crowds in the city,
My heart is wandering still, beguiled,
Gleaning the feel of the open country
With the wonder and joy of a little child.

Photo Opposite
RED BARN AND FIELD OF LUPINES
Franconia, New Hampshire
William Johnson
Johnson's Photography

Country Roads

Evelynn Merilatt Boal

I love a little country road,
A winding, wandering way,
One I can travel slowly
On a lovely summer day.

Across a rustic wooden bridge,
Beneath some touching trees,
With bittersweet along the fence
To gather if I please.

Away from sounds of traffic,
The pressure and the rush,
Where I can hear the meadowlark
And see a winging thrush.

I love a little country road
That comes from where it's been
And leads to some delightful place
Where I'm invited in.

QUIET COUNTRY ROAD
Vermont
Dianne Dietrich Leis, Photographer

Mountaintop

Mary E. Linton

Oh, I shall go remembering blue mist
And how the smoke curls in the valley there,
And some far day I will again keep tryst
With mountain solitude and pine-filled air.

And when I stand again, my feet in snow,
My head in drifting clouds swept like a gale,
With summer just a breathless glimpse below,
And Life still pointing to some higher trail,
I shall remember that this climb was good
And bless each mountaintop where I have stood.

I know, whatever all the years may bring,
Whatever changes there may be in me,
These peaks will be the same, and I shall sing,
Knowing a certain wild stability.

Photo Opposite
SUMMER PEAK
Mt. Ranier, Washington
Ed Cooper Photography

Photo Overleaf
MOUNTAINSIDE PASTURE
Wilson Peak, Colorado
Bob Clemenz Photography

Desert's Flower

Richard Summerhill

No other loves the rain
As much as desert's flower.
Its season over, it lays its grain
And awaits the next year's shower.

Cloistered in the earth,
Always waiting for the time
When rain begets its birth,
Grows, blossoms, then's supine.

As all things live and pass
And their schedules have been run,
Their time of joy is measured
And metered by the sun.

No desert flower knows the grace
Of life and joy each day.
Their splendid blossom's pace
Is one year and rain away.

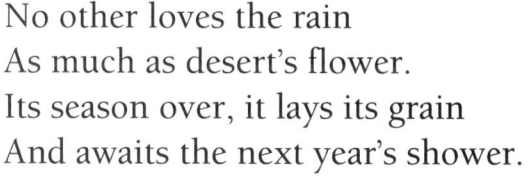

Photo Opposite
MEXICAN GOLDPOPPY AND OWL CLOVER BLOSSOMS
Organ Pipe National Monument, Arizona
Dick Dietrich Photography

WONDER

Joy Belle Burgess

There's a wonder that shines
On the roll of the waves
When a little girl meets the sea,
When she runs with delight in the bubbly foam
And the ripples bright and free.

There's a magic that rides
On the wings of the wind
When a little boy feels the spray,

SUMMER SURF
Nags Head, North Carolina
Dan Dempster, Photographer

As he frolics and breathes the fresh salt air
In his moments of carefree play.

There's a lively joy that sings in her heart
When a little girl hears the cry
Of a low-flying gull that glides on the wind
Against the blue of the sky.

There's a wonder that shines
On the roll of the waves
As they break on the sand wild and free,
And joy is the song that sings
In his heart
When a little boy meets the sea.

TESTING THE WIND
San Diego, California
Dianne Dietrich Leis, Photographer

A Little Old Place

Douglas Malloch

A little old farm near some little old town!
Well, leave it to me and I'd settle right down
In some little old house on some little old place;
Then, city, good-bye, for I'm out of the race.
For I figure a man could be fairly content,
Though the city might say that he hadn't a cent,
With a cow in the barn and a pig in the pen
And a horse and a dog and occasional hen.

If I could have my way, I'd look till I found
Some little old place with some posies around,
A little old house setting back from the pike
Where all I would do would be do what I like.
I figure a man would be willing to toil
With a horse and a dog and a bit of the soil,
A woman be willing to cook and to darn
With a pig in the pen and a cow in the barn.

So if somewhere some farmer is sick of his life,
His children unhappy, unhappy his wife,
If somewhere the roses no longer are sweet
And someone is longing for pavements and heat,
I gladly will trade you my job and my flat;
For I think I could really be happy, at that,
With a cow in the barn and a pig in the pen
And a horse and a dog and occasional hen.

Things with a Country Flavor

Edna Jaques

Things with a country flavor:
    June butter yellow as gold,
A little spring in the milk house
    Whose waters are glacier cold.

Buttermilk thick and creamy,
    Sweet from a wooden churn,
Fresh baked bread from a country stove
    Done to a golden turn.

Homemade cider in wooden kegs
    Aged like the rarest wine,
A cantelope cold as the morning air
    Plucked from a dew-wet vine.

Pickles made from old recipes
    Handed down through the years,
Mother and daughter keeping faith
    With the best of the pioneers.

Home-raised pork in a salty brine,
    Potatoes warm from a hill,
Holding the flavor of common earth
    Under their jackets still.

Things with a country flavor:
    Corn in a rainproof shock,
A country kitchen at suppertime,
    The smell of a sun-warmed rock.

Photo Opposite
SUMMER'S BOUNTY
Ralph Luedtke, Photographer

50 YEARS AGO

Country Barn and Swimming Pond.

Stark Lines in a Mellow Landscape

The beauty of the unstudied architecture of the farmhouses and farm buildings throughout our land is a delight to the eye of the average wayfarer as well as to that of the more critical and discriminating artist. From the rockstrewn hillsides of New England to the mountainous corrugations of Colorado, one views delightful compositions of house and barn, silo, woodshed and corn crib, all contributing to a natural, functional architecture, untouched by any product of the Beaux Arts or of the modernistic school.

In New England, an architectural heritage exists of white clapboard houses and dooryard gardens, shadowed by ancient elms, with old, weathered barns mellowed like a well-thumbed book. There they stand as mute evidence that whoever built them builded well and with a keen sense of proportion. The early builders had few, if any, books to guide them. Therefore their aesthetic principles were of the most primitive sort. They placed their buildings in a simple but appropriate arrangement, with agreeable outlines, and then succeeding generations added a rambling queue of ells, sheds, and outbuildings, which were sort of an architectural genealogy of the inhabitants through the years. Surprising as it may be, in most cases each part is in due proportion to the whole and in proper relation to it.

In the olden times it was a blessing that most of the detail was made by hand; therefore it was used sparingly, if at all. It is a fact that a simple barn utterly devoid of embellishment has artistic qualities of form and composition, which would be entirely lost were it smothered in a maze of detail or ornament.

Whether he called himself that or not, the hand of the landscape architect is evident around the early farmsteads. The wisteria-covered shingles, the lilac in the dooryard, and the haphazard use of stone walls contributed a charm which landscape architects of today may well envy.

New England is not alone in her rural architectural heritage. Throughout the rolling farmlands of Pennsylvania one sees examples of the early builders' handiwork in the stone houses, barns, and cook ovens. Even the simplest woodshed, corn crib, or milkhouse presents a fascinating aspect. If the difficulty of producing ornamentation was one blessing in disguise, the necessity of using local materials was another. Where in New England the simple clapboards, shingles, or plain boarding were used, here in Pennsylvania thick stone walls with wide, white joints possessed a charming quality wholly indigenous to the region. It is this use of natural materials, used in a natural way, which contributed so much to the beauty of the farm buildings of yesterday. Much as the machine has given us in comfort, its products are inclined to be cold and harsh, and set, whereas those materials which possess the local craftsman's touch possess charm and quality in themselves alone.

Throughout the broad prairies of Kansas, Idaho, and Oklahoma are more modern examples of farmsteads, happy in their composition and tranquil in their surroundings. Although the more modern layouts lack the mellowness of age, the various buildings necessary for their several uses present such an endless variety of groupings that the results are picturesque in the extreme. What better picture could a Grant Wood paint than sheer white silos silhouetted against a cerulean sky, with endless plains stretching to the horizon? From the lake-strewn surfaces of Minnesota to the mountainous valleys of Montana and Nevada are architectural masterpieces, generally unheralded and unsung.

Perhaps the agricultural appeal to the farm is more than its buildings alone. It may well be in the cattle and fields, the sun-baked hay in the meadows, or in the girdle of trees, dark green behind the gleaming white of the farmhouse walls. There is a little bit of the farmer in most of us; the lure of the soil is strong. That is why our suburban houses of today are affected by the farmhouse architecture of yesterday. Doctors, lawyers, cobblers, and candlestick makers who cannot live in the country try to bring the farm to themselves by building copies of farmhouses in the suburbs. Whether you like it or not, this is the sincerest flattery to the aesthetic quality of our farm buildings.

This year, hundreds of city dwellers are actually going back to the farms. They are urged by the feeling of security that lies in the soil. Some will succeed in their venture and others will fail. The measure of their success will depend to no small degree on the planning of their farm buildings, or in the most advantageous use of the buildings at hand. Good farm architecture is, of course, more than a romantic red barn on a hilltop. It means good planning and efficient use of space; it means scientific study and careful design of each building for its particular use and its relation to the group as a whole. There are hidden possibilities of design in any farm, new or old, that only await discovery by the architect who knows how to use them.

Printed in The Christian Science Monitor, *June 5, 1943.*

Country Lane and Farm.

Gray Barns and Grandfathers

Ralph W. Seager

North country barns stand weathered and gray,
Smoothed by the rub of sandpaper years.
    Their boards are uncolored,
      No paint on the grain,
Except where the wind has brushed in the rain.

The meadows in summer ride up to these lofts
Where incense is mingled warm with the touch
    Of spice from the horses
      And sweetness from cows
As June and July are piled in the mows.

This is the time these barns look their best,
Doors flung wide open to welcome the fields.
    Gray is the goodness
      Brought out by the weather;
Gray barns and grandfathers look good together.

NORTH COUNTRY BARN
Near Lincoln, Massachusetts
Dianne Dietrich Leis, Photographer

Grandpa Happy's Cabin at Gobbler's Knob.

Grandpa Happy

Cheryl Tenbrook

Mother called him "Daddy," to Grandmother he was "Myron," my cousins called him "Grandfather," and when I was young, I called him "Pawkee," my childish mispronunciation of "Grandpa." But to the neighbors around Gobbler's Knob, he was known as "Happy."

My grandfather was called "Happy" for good reason. He was a happy man, at ease with himself and the world. I think he enjoyed being a bit of a character. He waved at every man, woman, child, and dog that passed by his place and usually shouted a loud "How do!" If anyone stopped by for a visit, he'd say, "Howdy neighbor, come set and rest yourself on the porch." His parting words were always, "Come back when ya got time to stay—glad you got to see me!"

Most evenings after dinner, Grandpa would go outside the cabin and let out a holler to wake the dead. If one of us grandkids dared to look a little quizzical, he'd say, with a straight face but a twinkle in his eye, "Pardon me, madam, I'm just sayin' howdy to the neighbors. That's the way we kept in touch with one another in the old days, don't cha' know." I always thought he was pulling my leg until one night he hollered, and I'll be switched if some old boy down the road didn't holler right back.

When it was dark, Grandpa Happy would call up the whippoorwills for us. First, he'd "whip-o-will, whip-o-will," and way off in the valley below we'd barely hear the birds' reply. He'd call again, and the birds would come closer until finally they would fly to the giant oak just over the roof of the cabin.

In the daytime, Grandpa taught us how to whistle to the bobwhites and get them to talk. He seemed like "the old man of the mountain" to me. He searched through the sumac and May apples to find where the pawpaws grew, and then he would cut open the creamy yellowish flesh for us to eat. He harvested black walnuts, wild strawberries, blackberries, and morel mushrooms from the woods. He stole to a secret location each spring to cut sassafras roots to make tea to "thin our blood." He found us chestnuts to carry in our pockets for luck and whittled us whistles out of willow wood. After the first hard frost, Grandpa would bring in soft orange persimmons. I never really developed an appreciation for their pungent flavor, but as a little girl, I loved to have Grandpa Happy cut open the seeds to see if there were a "knife," "fork," or "spoon" inside.

Grandpa Happy lived by a work ethic that is fast vanishing from our culture. He gave a full day's work for a fair day's wage, and then he returned home and did several more hours of chores. He was always ready to help a neighbor. He paid cash for what he could afford and did without the rest. He made do, used things up, and wore things out.

A deep and abiding faith in God directed Grandpa Happy's life. When he prayed, it sounded to me like God was Grandpa's most personal friend. Every Sunday morning he'd be up and dressed in his best suit ready to head off to Fairview or Berryman Baptist Church or some other little chapel nearby to "lead the sangin'." Sometimes Mom and Dad and I would go with him, and sometimes we would use "vacation" as an excuse to head for the river with our fishing poles. Grandpa would heatedly wish us bad luck; he hoped we'd catch "nary a fish," and he'd go on his way. He allowed as how God didn't take any vacations from church, we shouldn't either.

Grandpa Happy sang with joy and enthusiasm. A trained musician would point out that his voice was nasal and he was too loud; but Grandpa began singing long before the days of microphones, and he wanted to be sure the ladies in the back pew heard every word. And they did.

There just aren't many folks left like Grandpa Happy; their generation is all but closed, but Grandpa left my cousins and me a rich heritage. He taught us how to track deer and chop wood. He brought us up on spring water and taught us to steer clear of poison oak; but he taught us so much more than that. He taught us values: to be honest, work hard, put God first, love your neighbor, be happy. I'll always feel deeply rooted in the Ozarks because of Grandpa. Those rocky hills were so much a part of him, and now they are a part of me too. Whenever I hear the whippoorwills call at dusk, I think of the man who wanted no more than a simple, honest life in a small cabin on a hill in an Ozark forest. And I know just how lucky I am that Happy was my grandfather.

My Grandpa

Kay Hoffman

My grandpa has the nicest face,
The biggest, warmest smile;
But most of all, I like the best
My grandpa's homespun style.

My grandpa taught me how to fish
And where the big trout run;
And though his tales were sometimes tall,
He made the day such fun!

So many things my grandpa taught
That make my life worthwhile:
Warm companionship and kindness
And folks are meant to smile.

Handmade Heirloom

Dark Iris tied by Preston Jennings. Photo courtesy of The American Museum of Fly Fishing, Manchester, Vermont. Photo by Linda M. Golder.

Atlantic Salmon Flies

Heidi King

Rat-faced McDougal, Blue Charm, Dark Iris, Silver Gray, Thunder and Lightning, Black Dose, Grey Ghost, Orange Fish Hawk—these colorful names accurately describe the detailed replicas of aquatic insects known as Atlantic salmon flies. Often containing an intricate mixture of feathers from ten or more exotic birds found on three or four different continents, these handcrafted lures are considered by many to be the most ornate and appealing artificial flies ever fashioned.

As early as the fifteenth century, anglers in Europe were catching salmon on artificial flies made from the ordinary plumes of snipe, partridge, and bittern. In the mid-seventeenth century, however, Richard Franck, a soldier in Oliver Cromwell's army, concluded that a salmon "delights in the most gaudy and Orient colors you can choose." When he recommended tying flies from the feathers of chicken, peacock, pheasant, mallard, teal, parrot, heron, parakeet, flamingo, and macaw, the craft became an art

form in which fly dressers competed to design the most intricate and colorful patterns.

During the Victorian era, extravagant flies increased in popularity. Because of the exotic plumage used, the flies became instant status symbols, and fishing was elevated from a mere sport to a royal pastime. British sailors returning from worldwide voyages imported feathers from the many exotic ports they visited to satisfy the increased demand and supplement their meager wages. Shrewd fly dressers befriended sea captains who allowed them to barter for the feathers instead of paying an outright sum.

The art of salmon fly tying never reached the same heights in the United States as it did in Europe. Only those who could afford the imported feathers actually turned this craft into a desirable pastime. Additionally, fishing, like hunting, was considered part of the frontier ethic, to be practiced only for survival. Conservation acts in the nineteenth and twentieth centuries also limited fly tying by regulating the slaughter of birds for plumage, prohibiting the interstate transportation of songbirds, and forbidding the importation of feathers of most wild birds.

Despite the limitations today, American fly dressers are still creating classic lures for their elaborate patterns and nostalgic value. Flies rivaling those of the Victorian age have cleverly evolved into masterpieces created from native duck and pheasant feathers, hair from mules or white-tailed deer, straight elk hair, spun Angora wool, and yarn, all dyed to match the exotic feathers they are replacing. Tinsel is sometimes added to give the fly an extra flash as it glides through the water.

Just like traditional Victorian flies, modern Atlantic salmon flies are the epitome of functional beauty. Each material used has a specific purpose and is strategically placed to give the fly optimal movement. Combining the fluffy fibers found at the base of a feather's hackle stem with normal hackle fibers gives an artificial fly durability and maximum movement. Black bear hairs wound around a silver pheasant crest feather top some flies for added shine.

The size of the fly and the number of hooks are important considerations when tying salmon flies. Larger flies are more effective in high, fast, or dirty water; smaller sizes should be used in midsummer when the water is low and clear. Single-hook flies work well in slow water, but the extra weight of double-hook flies is needed when fishing in rapid currents.

Choosing colors is an essential aspect of fly tying, and most fly dressers agree that bright colors—green, yellow, and orange—attract salmon. The rule of thumb is "bright day, bright fly; dark day, dark fly." The riverbed and water's color also determine what color fly to use because each may affect the visibility of particular colors.

Regardless of the many factors determining a salmon fly's design, its ornate beauty and efficient designs remain as fascinating today as in the nineteenth century.

Heidi King makes her home in Tallahassee, Florida, and loves all arts and crafts.

Grey Ghost tied by Carrie Stevens.
Photo courtesy of The American Museum of Fly Fishing.
Photo by Linda M. Golder.

Prayer for a New Father

Reginald Holmes

I gaze at him with wondering eyes
As in his mother's arms he lies.
So small is he, and yet so sweet;
So big the world he comes to greet.

Yet in those little hands I see
The shape and form of things to be,
The blueprint of a world somehow
That's far better than we know now.

Help me to meet the challenge hurled
With my son's entrance to this world.
Give me the knowledge, courage, skill
To teach him how to do Thy will.

And let there flow from my two hands
The strength he needs and life demands.
Let me be kind, yet firm and wise,
And with the hope that in me lies,
God, let me do the best I can
To help my son become a man.

I Have a Boy

Hugh M. Pierce

I've a wonderful boy, and I say to him, "Son,
Be fair and be square in the race you must run.
Be brave if you lose and be meek if you win;
Be better and nobler than I've ever been.
Be honest and noble in all that you do,
And honor the name I have given to you."

I have a boy, and I want him to know
We reap in life just about as we sow;
And we get what we earn, be it little or great,
Regardless of luck and regardless of fate.
I will teach him and show the best that I can
That it pays to be honest and upright, a man.

I will make him a pal and a partner of mine
And show him the things in this world that are fine.
I will show him the things that are wicked and bad,
For I figure this knowledge should come from his dad.
I will walk with him, talk with him, play with him, too;
And to all of my promises strive to be true.

We will grow up together; I'll too be a boy
And share in his trouble and share in his joy.
We'll work out our problems together, and then
We will lay our plans when we both will be men.
And, oh, what a wonderful joy this will be;
No pleasure in life could be greater to me.

Photo Opposite
FATHER AND SON
Original painting by John Walter

A SLICE OF LIFE
— Edgar A. Guest —

Why Fathers Boast

Little girl, just half past two,
    With those laughing eyes of blue
And that smirk of mirth and gladness
    And that flash of mischief, too,
Can you tell just what your dad is
    Thinking of, and just how glad is
That old heart of his this minute
    To be looking down on you?

Other little girls have eyes
    Just as sparkling with surprise;
There are countless other babies
    Just as mischievous and wise;

But to me, I swear 'tis true,
    Not another one would do;
There's no baby in this wide world
    Quite so wonderful as you!

You have something, I suppose,
    Not another baby knows,
I could pick you from ten millions
    By the wrinkles on your toes;
By that something extra fine,
    I should say almost divine,
By that radiant lovely spirit
    I should know that you were mine.

Little girl, just half past two,
    Though I boast the charms of you,
That is something every other
    Doting daddy here will do;
Just as I fill up with pride,
    Every daddy, far and wide,
With the baby God has sent him,
    Is supremely satisfied.

So I'm telling this to you,
    Little girl, just half past two,
That you'll not grow over boastful
    Of the foolish things I do;
North and south, and east and west,
    By this fancy we're possessed.
Every dad, the world wide over,
    Thinks his babe the very best.

Edgar A. Guest began his illustrious career in 1895 at the age of fourteen when his work first appeared in the Detroit Free Press. *His column was syndicated in over 300 newspapers, and he became known as "The Poet of the People."*

LITTLE FARMER BOY

Beatrice Godby Goble

It seems but only yesterday
I watched a toddler out at play;
With spade and hoe, on dimpled knees,
My two-year old was "planting trees."

And then how fast the moments run;
A four-year old, nut-browned by sun,
On pedal tractor, calls out, "Now
I'll help my daddy with the plow."

In wind and sun, through passing years,
A boy grows quickly, it appears;
With tractor chugging down the lane,
Today a youth will cut the grain.

Dad stands to watch then heaves a sigh,
"He's young, but he is bound to try.
I must admit our son has grown;
Guess he can manage on his own!"

And though I'm proud and very glad
He'll do the job as well as Dad,
There's sorrow mingled with my joy;
I miss my little farmer boy.

A BASKET'S WORTH OF WORK
Art Phaneuf
New England Stock Photo

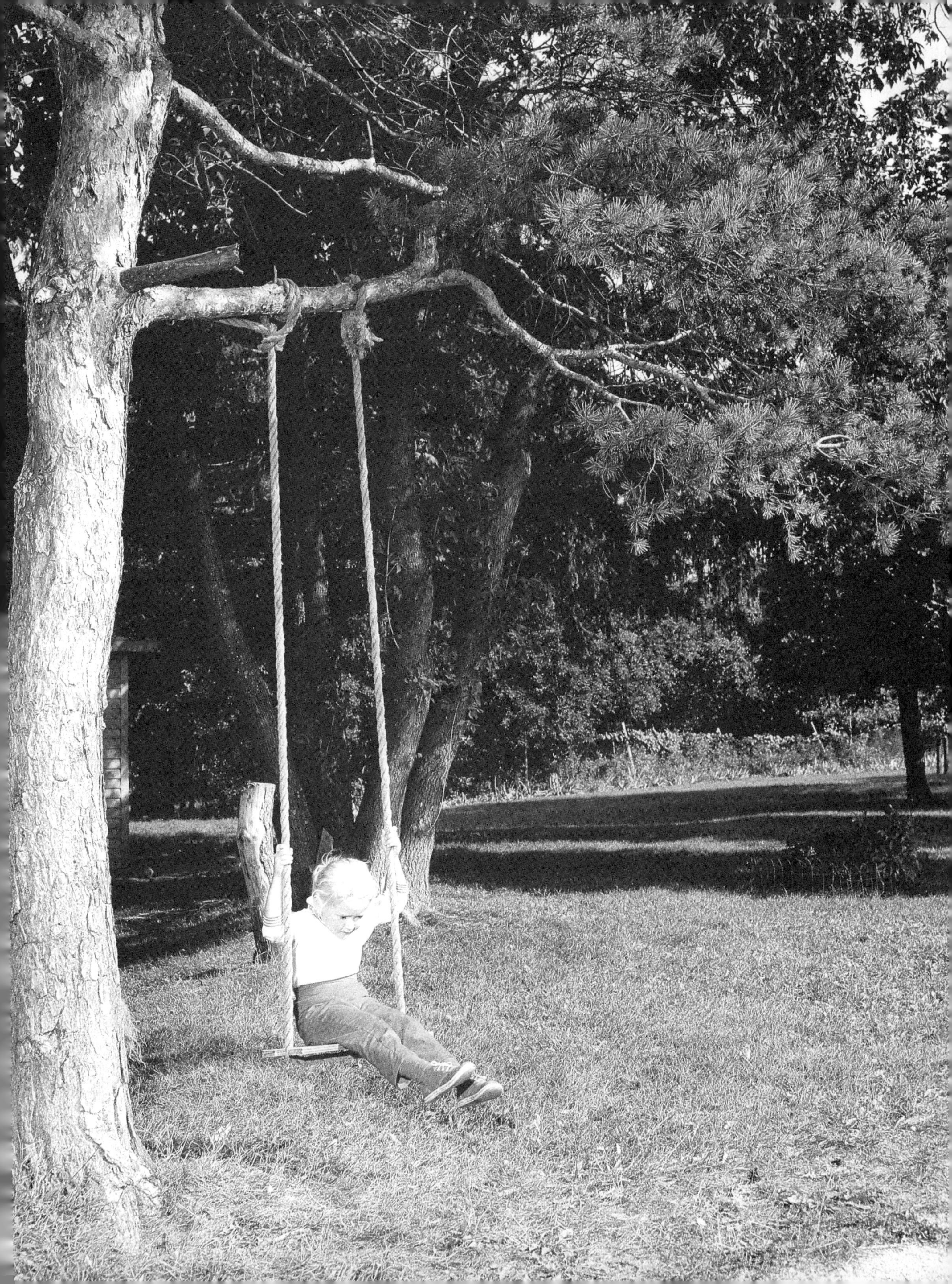

Seven and Five and Three

Jessie Tillman-Orphey

Do you remember the old rope swing
That Papa built in the evergreen tree
Where the summer breeze drifted
And sparrows would sing
When we were seven and five and three?

And can you remember the miniature stream
That flowed 'neath the tree so tall,
The one Mama made to water her dream
When summer was long and rain didn't fall?

And do you remember our "mulberry" feet,
Small bodies near bare, toasted brown?
And recall if you will the nightshade's perfume
That rose on the mist as the sun went down.

I'm caught in a bubble of memory,
The swing, the stream, and the tree,
When we thought time was ours
And we'd never be older
Than seven and five and three.

For the Children

Artwork by Russ Flint

In the Garden

Ernest Crosby

I spied beside the garden bed
    A tiny lass of ours
Who stopped and bent her sunny head
    Above the red June flowers.

Pushing the leaves and thorns apart,
    She singled out a rose
And in its inmost crimson heart,
    Enraptured, plunged her nose.

"O dear, dear rose, come, tell me true,
    Come, tell me true," said she,
"If I smell just as sweet to you
    As you smell sweet to me!"

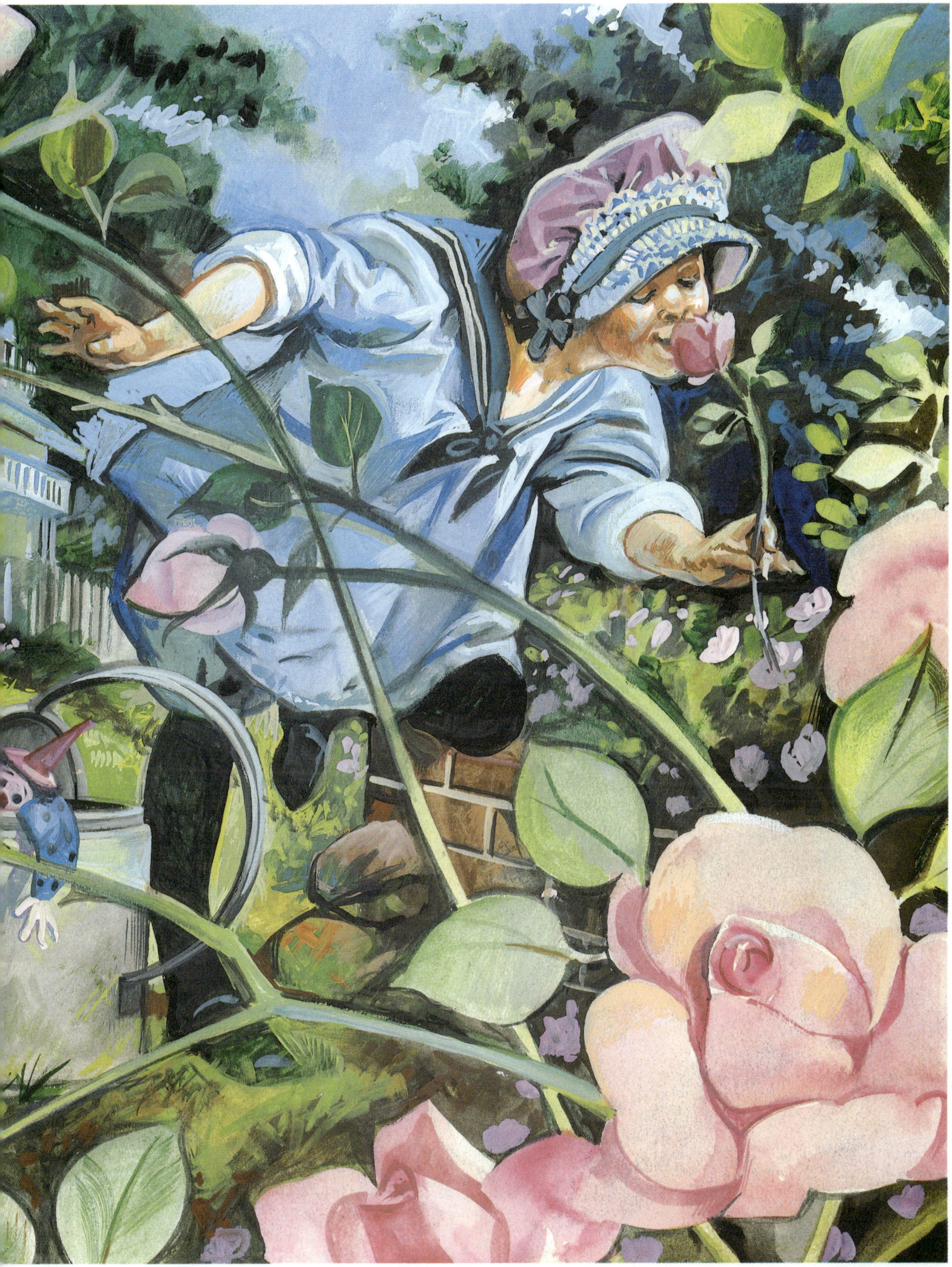

Readers' Reflections

Editor's Note: Readers are invited to submit unpublished, original poetry for possible publication in future issues of *Ideals*. Please send copies only; manuscripts will not be returned. Writers receive $10 for each published submission. Send material to "Readers' Reflections," Ideals Publishing Corporation, P.O. Box 140300, Nashville, TN 37214-0300. For an upcoming special edition, *Ideals* is looking for first-hand accounts of life in America before the twentieth century. Readers are invited to share family diaries, journals, letters, and other accounts of life before the turn of the century. Please submit material to the above address, ATTN: "Heritage of America." Send copies only; manuscripts cannot be returned.

The Blue Jay

The blue jay in the valley,
He told me secret things,
Of the music in his feathers
And how the sunbeam sings;
And the way of dancing shadows
He told me with his wings.

The blackbird flies with panic,
The swallow goes with light,
The doves, they move like ladies,
The owl floats by at night;
But the great and flashing blue jay,
He swoops as fliers might.

The hawk is cruel and rigid;
He watches from the heights.
The crow is slow and somber;
The robin loves a fight;
But the joyous, flashing blue jay,
He flies as heroes fight.

The sparrow flits unthinking
And twitters on his flight;
The heron trails his legs behind;
The lark climbs out of sight;
But the singing, flashing blue jay,
He soars as poets might.

Andy Marshall
New London, New Hampshire

Garden Guest

I hear you, little hummingbird;
Your sound is quite alarming!
Now that I see you're not a bee,
Your presence here is charming!

As you invade my flower bed
With ruby throat a-blazing,
You hover, dip, and dart about;
Your flight path is amazing!

I watch your midair pirouette,
Which gives me cause to ponder,
What powers your remote control?
Indeed, you are a wonder!

Now quickly as you came, you leave.
You've touched on every flower
And won my admiration with
Your mighty "hummer" power.

            Eleanor Christensen
            Penn Yan, New York

Evening in the Country

The sun has lately gone to rest
    Behind a purple hill.
Some distant music tinkles
    From our little rocky rill.

The four-o'clocks along the path
    Have opened dainty bells,
And from the hill the whippoorwill
    His evening message tells.

A mellow light will soon be shed
    By a peeping yellow moon,
As cricket concerts in the lane
    Their drowsy ditties croon.

The countryside is so serene;
    And blessed, I kneel and pray
For all the world to know such peace
    As the close of this summer day.

            Mary Simmons
            Hillsboro, Ohio

FROM MY GARDEN JOURNAL

Deana Deck

WILD BLACKBERRIES. FPG International.

Easy-pickin' Blackberries

It's a safe guess that nearly everyone who has grown up outside a city shares a common childhood memory. The time is a hot, sunny day in early summer; the place is somewhere along a country road or the side of a hill where tall bushes grow heavy with black, sweet, ripe fruit waiting to be collected in a pail or sack, or sometimes just a pocket or cap. I remember lots of juicy sampling and stained clothing that Mom had to get after with the bleach. As kids, we always knew that summer was really here when blackberry-picking time arrived.

There's another part of the memory, however, that most of us omit when we're feeling nostalgic for childhood's summer pleasures: the thorns. Nothing grabbed clothing and snared tender skin quite like the nasty barbs that lurked on a wild blackberry bush. I suspect those thorns are one reason few of us venture out to collect wild blackberries anymore, or, for that matter, have a hedge of them growing alongside the yard the way many of our grandparents did.

Since blackberries are very tender and difficult to ship, unless you grow your own, chances are you don't enjoy them very often. That means no paraffin-topped jars of homemade blackberry jam stacked in the cupboard and no summer evenings topped off with hot blackberry cobbler and ice cream—at least for some of us. I'm happy to report that I still indulge in these luxuries ever since I discovered the Chester Thornless Blackberry while thumbing through a garden catalog. I instantly ordered five plants and have never regretted it. Whoever invented this boon to mankind should be honored with a statue in the park, at the very least.

Thornless blackberries are hardy enough to be grown in all but a handful of northern states. They are highly productive and disease resistant, and, when kept properly pruned, produce berries every bit as sweet and juicy as the ones that haunt our memories. The only thing these bushes lack is thorns. Who needs 'em?

Blackberries are easy to grow. Be sure to purchase plants that are certified virus-free, and plant them in early spring in full sun. Water them well in dry weather, especially during the first year, using a soaker hose rather than a sprinkler to prevent mildew. Mulching with compost will limit weeds, conserve soil moisture, and add ample nutrients to the soil.

Whether your canes have thorns or not, pruning is the key to success with blackberries. Thorny varieties, however, are so difficult to prune that most people postpone the chore from year to year until the berry yield is so poor they feel justified plowing the bushes under and replacing them with something more benign; happily, this is not the case with thornless varieties.

Most thornless blackberries grow similarly to the trailing varieties and do best when trained against a fence-like trellis. Mine grow along three rows of bamboo rails attached to sturdy uprights. This method saves space; my plants grow in an area two-feet wide and ten-feet long.

Blackberries produce fruit on second-season canes, meaning the new canes that sprout this summer will not bear fruit until next summer. Since the fruit tends to grow at the outermost tips of the canes, you can keep it within easy reach by pruning the plants the first year when they are about four-feet high and gently tying these canes to your trellis, wall, or fence. They will later sprout vigorous side shoots that will produce fruit the following season. These long canes can be woven in and out of your trellis during the summer to keep them looking attractive and tidy and to support the weight of the fruit the following summer. During the winter, trim these side shoots back to eighteen inches in length. This extra pruning will reduce the number of berries the plant produces; but never fear, you will have more berries than you can handle, and they will be larger than if you let the plant grow unattended.

Once a cane has produced berries, it will never bear again. Following the first frost at the end of the plant's second growing season, these canes will turn brown and are easy to recognize. In the fall, cut out these old canes—it's so easy when there are no thorns to contend with! The new shoots which appeared during the summer and which you will have pruned to a four-foot height can be tied to the trellis in place of the old canes you remove.

Trailing-type blackberries left to their own devices will "travel." If you do not prune them, the canes can reach twenty feet in length and will soon bend down to touch the ground. From this point, a new shoot will often appear since the tip that touches the ground is able to send out roots. Keeping the plants pruned is an easy solution to this spreading.

Some older gardening reference books caution that thornless varieties will produce shoots bearing thorns. This may have been true of the earlier varieties, but I have never had a thorny shoot appear, and I have been growing thornless blackberries for seven years.

Thornless blackberries have become widely available in most garden centers and from nearly all mail-order nurseries. Order a few, and start looking up those old cobbler recipes!

Deana Deck lives in Nashville, Tennessee, where her garden column is a regular feature in The Tennessean.

Ideals' Family Recipes

Favorite recipes from the *Ideals'* family of readers.

Editor's Note: If you would like us to consider your favorite recipe, please send a typed copy of the recipe along with your name and address to: *Ideals* Magazine, ATTN. Recipes, P.O. Box 140300, Nashville, TN 37214. We will pay $10 for each recipe used. Recipes cannot be returned.

BLACKBERRY COBBLER

Preheat oven to 350°. In a bowl, mix 1 cup of sugar and 1 beaten egg; beat until creamy. Add 3 tablespoons of shortening to the sugar and egg and beat well. In a second bowl, mix together 1½ cups of flour, 1 teaspoon of baking powder, and ½ teaspoon of salt. Add the flour mixture, alternating with ½ cup of milk, to the sugar mixture.

Place 3 cups of blackberries in a greased baking dish and sprinkle 1 teaspoon of sugar over blackberries. Pour batter over fruit and bake in a 350° oven for 30 minutes. Remove and let cool slightly. Serve with a scoop of vanilla ice cream.

Bonnie Olsen
Edmond, Oklahoma

DEEP-DISH PEACH-PEAR PIE

In a bowl, mix 1½ cups of flour and ½ teaspoon of salt. Add ½ cup of vegetable shortening and work it into the flour until the mixture resembles fresh bread crumbs. Sprinkle with water, 1 tablespoon at a time, and stir dough with a fork until the dough holds together. Shape the dough into a cake and roll it out on a lightly floured surface until it is ⅛-inch thick and large enough to cover the top of a 2-quart baking dish with 1 inch of overhang all around. Set the dough aside and cover with wax paper so it will not dry out.

Preheat oven to 425°. In an ungreased 2-quart baking dish, mix 4 cups of peeled, pitted peaches cut into eighths and 4 cups of peeled, cored pears cut into eighths. In a second mixing bowl, mix together ¾ cup of sugar, 3½ tablespoons of flour, ¼ teaspoon of nutmeg, ¼ teaspoon of cinnamon, and a dash of salt. Add ⅔ cup of cream to sugar mixture and toss in 2-quart baking dish with the peaches. Top peaches evenly with ¼ stick of butter cut into pats.

Drape dough over the peaches, leaving at least 1 inch of overhang all around. Press the dough into the dish around the edges and fold the overhang under itself to make a double-thick rim. Flute edges and cut 2 or 3 vents in the crust for steam to escape.

Bake the pie in 425° oven for about 1 hour until the juices are bubbling, the crust is golden, and the fruit is tender when pierced. (You may need to cover edges of crust with foil halfway through baking to prevent burning.) Remove the pie from the oven and let it cool. Serve warm. Makes 10 servings.

Leslie Anderson
Tullahoma, Tennessee

CHERRY DUMP CAKE

Preheat oven to 350°. Dump one 20-oz. can of crushed pineapple into an ungreased 9 x 13-inch casserole dish and spread evenly over bottom. Dump one 21-oz. can of cherry pie filling over pineapples and spread evenly. Dump one box of yellow cake mix over fruit and level off with a spoon. Cut one stick of butter into pats and spread evenly over top of cake mix. Bake in 350° oven for 1 hour.

Jeff Wyatt
Indianapolis, Indiana

PEA

RUGS and QUILTS
CATERING
GOURMET FOOD
GIFTS and CRAFTS
ANTIQUES

THE OLD GENERAL STORE

Elisabeth Weaver Winstead

The wooden sign, through years of wear,
Listed the goods we bought with care:
Mixing whisks and butter molds,
Cast-iron stoves for the days it's cold.

Sweet sorghum for a syrup cake,
Wooden handles for an old leaf rake,
Blue pie plates and strong pine tar,
Honey that filled a green glass jar.

Biscuit pans and fresh meat cutters,
Churns for making country butter,
Aladdin lamps and grinding mills,
Potted plants for windowsills.

Soda crackers and peppermint sticks,
Smoking tobacco and oil lamp wicks.
Old stores have many a tale to tell
Of loving friends who know us well.

Though time brings changes for us all,
Those happy days we still recall,
Bright smiles and greetings by the score
At the dear, old-fashioned general store.

NOTICES OF SUMMER
Peacham, Vermont
Dick Dietrich Photography

THROUGH MY WINDOW
Pamela Kennedy

The Variety Store

Having moved to the Washington, D.C., area last year, I was prepared to adapt to a faster-paced lifestyle. I certainly did not expect to take a step back in time, but step back I did at The Variety Store, a country-style shopping experience located halfway between the White House and Mount Vernon.

Founded by Charles "Ben" Vennell, The Variety Store is testimony to the old-fashioned notions that the customer is always right, shopping should be an adventure, and assistance should be readily available. Since opening day in 1958, Ben has instructed the salespeople in his store to carry notepads and jot down every item customers asked for but couldn't find. Using these notes, he ordered new stock, often flying in the face of professional distributors who warned, "You'll never sell it!" But sell it he did, and within six years, Ben tripled the store's size. It's still not large, but I can spend half a day roaming through the extra high, extra deep shelves, discovering things I thought I'd never find again!

My introduction to The Variety Store came when I asked a neighbor if she knew where I might find a replacement for a hurricane lamp chimney broken in our last move. "Have you tried The Variety Store?" she inquired.

"Which variety store?" I asked, expecting the name of a well-known national chain.

"The Variety Store," she patiently repeated, with instructions to go down the road about two miles and turn left.

Following her directions, I pulled into a nearly full parking lot under a simple marquee. The windows were crammed with displays of fabric and patterns, ceramic figures, doll house furniture, and plumbing supplies. Baskets of silk flowers and bundles of baby's breath crowded me as I entered, and the scents of cinnamon, lavender, and strawberry blended in an unusual potpourri. Baskets of every shape and size teetered in six-foot stacks hanging from the ceiling. This was a place where serious shopping took place! I forgot what I had come for and indulged myself by wandering up and down the aisles.

The stock at The Variety Store is eclectic and arranged in what the owner proudly calls "organized clutter." Every turn reveals an interesting and usually unrelated section of merchandise. After browsing through a fascinating selection of designer buttons, I approached the hardware aisle located just behind the display of men's underwear. Beyond the plumber's friends and the moth flakes, I found the glassware and ceramics, arranged not by style, but by color. Piñatas shaped like mermaids, bulls, and parrots dangled on strings overhead. A holiday aisle boasted everything you could want for the Fourth of July—wind socks, flags, streamers, paper plates, plastic cups, even red, white, and blue confetti in star shapes!

After an hour, I recalled my initial reason for visiting this wonderful place. "Do you have hurricane lamp chimneys?" I asked a gray-haired employee. She gave me a patient smile and led me to the rear of the store, stood like a proud mother, and gestured upward in a sweeping arc—it was hurricane chimney heaven! On long shelves high above us stood hundreds of chimneys in orderly rows. The plain ones I wanted came in four different heights priced from $4.95-$8.98. After making my purchase at the cluttered check-out desk, I drove home satisfied and just a bit nostalgic.

I have since become a frequent customer at The Variety Store, where the unofficial slogan is: "If we don't have it, you don't need it!" Of course, sometimes I'm not sure exactly what I need, and that's when the well-trained Variety Store crew comes into play. Many of them have worked at the store for two decades, they're all as friendly as the folks next door, and most are just as likely to share an unsolicited opinion or two.

Once when I came in with a cocktail dress that needed a bit of reinforcement, I was pondering two different types of beaded trim to use as straps when the clerk in the fabric department eyed the frock and trim. "Well," she offered critically, "you could use those, but you'd end up looking like a piece of upholstered furniture." Having made that somewhat daunting comment, she led me to a perfectly matched bolt of tiny satin cording and instructed me to braid three strands together to make delicate straps. Then she also suggested what color hose and shoes would look best. This lady knew her stuff—and wasn't afraid to share it!

Just the other day, while I was waiting to purchase an item, I overheard a customer commenting that the white bamboo birdcage in the size she wanted was hanging on display and decorated with flowers and ribbons that wouldn't match her decor. No problem. The clerk dragged out a ladder, unhooked the birdcage, ripped off the offending decor, and handed over the cage with a smile. This kind of service is one reason why The Variety Store's customers are so loyal.

Young parents who grew up savoring weekly trips to The Variety Store now bring their children by to spend their allowances on penny candy and toys still priced under $1.00. I have watched my own daughter tightly clutching a handful of change and agonizing over sparkle bracelets, plastic jumping bugs, rubber snakes, and dozens of other temptations all well within her meager price range.

The Variety Store is more than just a place to spend some cash; it's a walk back in time, a place to feel the wonder of abundance, a place to relive some memories. It is what stores used to be "when we were kids" and there were innumerable items available for under $1.00.

As I sat talking with the proprietor the other day, our conversation was interrupted by the telephone's ring. "Maracas?" he repeated, "sure, we got 'em. I'll put a pair up by the cash register for you." It's great to know there is still a place where you can find what you need and be treated the good old-fashioned way.

Pamela Kennedy is a freelance writer of short stories, articles, essays, and children's books. Married to a naval officer and mother of three children, she has made her home on both U.S. coasts and in Hawaii and currently resides in Washington, D.C. She draws her material from her own experiences and memories, adding bits of her imagination to create a story or mood.

COLLECTOR'S CORNER

Tim Hamling

Francis Scott Key's Star Spangled Banner that flew at Fort McHenry in 1814 now hangs in the National Museum of American History.

Flag Memorabilia

The Fourth of July offers the perfect opportunity for flag enthusiasts to display their star-spangled banners, but for flag collectors, displaying their colors is a year-round passion. In addition to actual flags, collectors eagerly seek any items bearing the stars-and-stripes motif. Quilts, jewelry, and political memorabilia are all popular items that have been used to showcase the American flag.

Flags appeal to collectors for two primary reasons: historical interest and patriotism. Since American flags can be dated by their stars, collectors can immediately identify their flag's historical context. Ever since the first U.S. flag appeared in the late eighteenth century, a variety of designs have been used to display the stars-and-stripes. This variety is due to the vaguely worded Flag Resolution of 1777, which stated "that the flag of the United States be thirteen stripes, alternate red and white; that the Union be thirteen stars, white in a blue field, representing a new constellation." The Resolution, how-

54

ever, did not specify the stars' arrangement or their shape; consequently, flag makers created various imaginative designs for the field of stars, such as wreath and "great star" patterns.

As new states joined the Union, additional stars were added and new designs appeared. Thirty-four-star flags from the Civil War period are among the more popular designs. Unfortunately, they are often duplicated, and imitations are abundant. Collectors should be particularly wary; claims that holes and stains are the result of bullets and blood are usually false.

In addition to false documentation, commemorative flags produced for centennial celebrations can make identifying authentic flags more difficult. These replicas are obviously not as valuable as the originals, which can be priced as high as $1000 for late nineteenth-century designs. Older flags are priced even higher, but collectors should study a flag thoroughly to verify its authenticity before purchasing it. Authentic flags with fewer than thirty-six stars are very rare, and authentic flags with fewer than twenty-six stars are virtually nonexistent.

Patriotic fervor accounts for the great number of flag designs found on a wide variety of items. Flag designs for quilts seem a natural development due to the popularity of both. Quilters, however, took great liberties with their designs, often adding elements that never appeared on American flags, although most quilts incorporated the stars-and-stripes motif. These quilts, if dated, can be priced much higher than their flag counterparts, often over $10,000.

Jewelry, particularly lapel pins, is a popular item for the flag motif. Designs usually take the shape of a wind-blown banner bearing the stars-and-stripes arrangement. These items, however, are valued by the gems used to make them, not their resemblance to actual flags. Rhinestone studded pins are quite affordable, but others using rubies, sapphires, and diamonds become extremely expensive.

Flags lend themselves perfectly to political memorabilia. Banners, buttons, hats, and other items display a patriotic fervor in addition to supporting a particular candidate. In comparison to actual flags and flag quilts, these items are relatively inexpensive, ranging from a few dollars to a few hundred dollars.

Authentic flags and flag memorabilia can often be found at estate sales, Americana sales, and auctions; but the best method of adding to collections is networking with other collectors who can help locate and verify the authenticity of desired items. As the number of flag fanatics continues to grow, every day looks more and more like the Fourth of July.

Mid-nineteenth-century flag quilt honoring the 1876 Centennial Exhibition at Fairmount Park in Philadelphia, Shelburne Museum, Shelburne, Vermont. Photograph by Ken Burris.

TREASURES

Barbara W. Weber

While some may keep their treasures
Secured by sturdy locks,
I hoard my prized possessions
In a simple cardboard box.

There you'll find a family picture
From my childhood days of yore,
And wrapped about with tissue,
The first shoes my baby wore.

A precious old love letter
With which I would never part;
Though the words are dim and faded,
They're still written on my heart.

So many yellowed clippings
That recall both pain and joy.
There's a happy proclamation
That announces, "It's a boy!"

The corsage of white carnations
That I've pressed and laid away
Brings a flood of happy memories
Of my daughter's wedding day.

"Dear Mom," says a child's letter,
"Thank-you for the treat we had."
And there are welcomed weekly letters
Through the years from Mom and Dad.

And the annual Christmas greetings
That my loved ones always send,
And a thirty-year-old letter
From a special college friend.

When my inventory's finished
And I close my treasure chest,
Then my heart is filled with wonder
At the wealth with which I'm blessed.

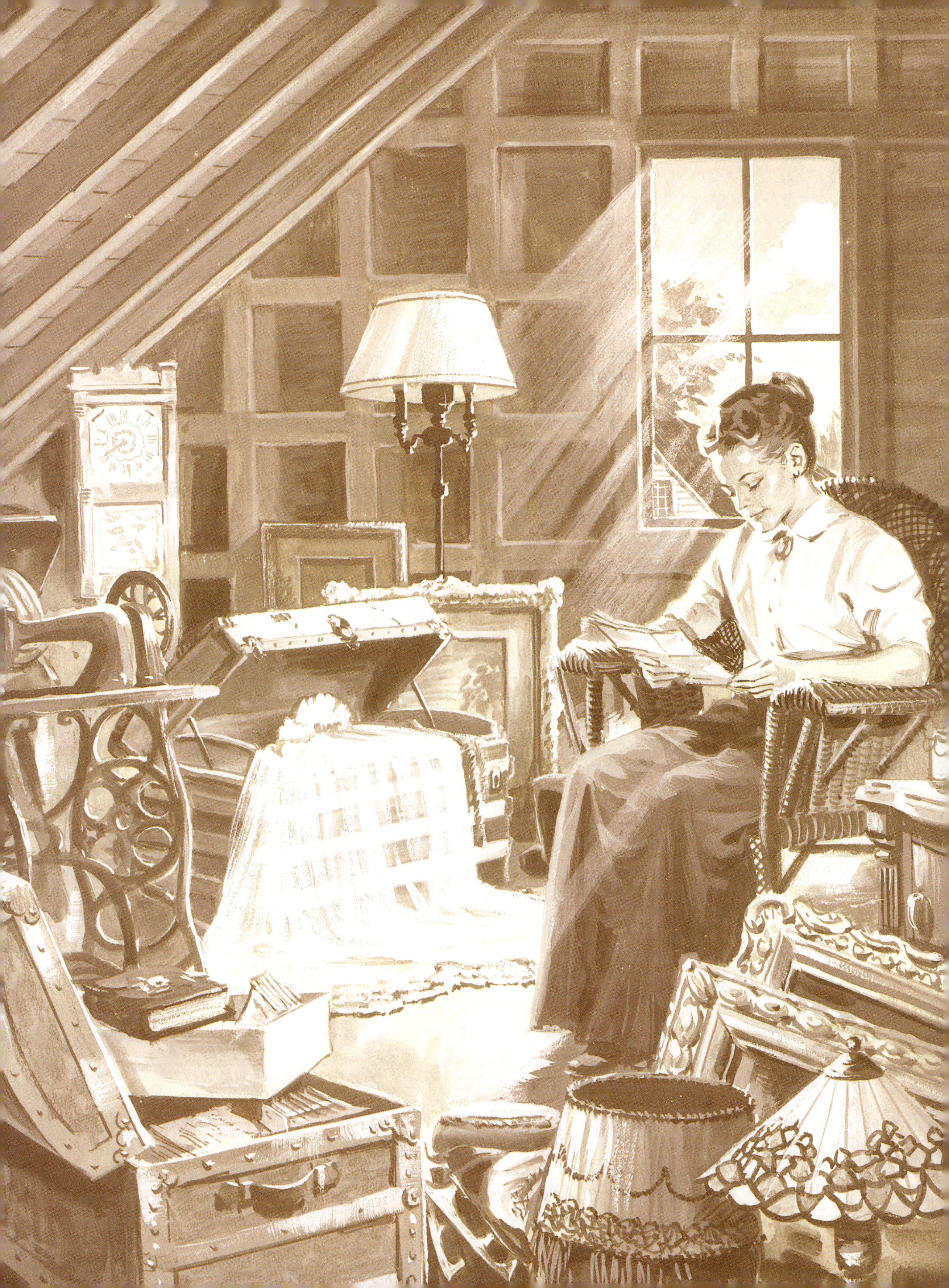

We the
insure domestic Tranquility,
and our Posterity,
Article. 1
Section. 1. All legislative Powers
Section. 2.

Freedom's Quest

Ruby Phillipy

They came, the weary and oppressed,
To this fair land, untamed and new;
They came in freedom's noble quest
With faith in God to guide them through.

They settled down where fortune led,
And axe strokes echoed loud and clear
As ageless silence heard the tread
Of brave and zealous pioneers.

They built log homes of sturdy wood
And hewed by hand their rugged way;
And all they did was strong and good,
With dauntless courage for each day.

The land produced abundant gain,
And stable progress spanned the years;
Great cities spawned on hills and plain
As vision broadened our frontiers.

Our flag flies on with pride and grace;
The heritage we emulate
Will not be bound by time or space,
For freedom makes our nation great.

SYMBOLS OF FREEDOM
FPG International

The Stars and Stripes Forever

John Philip Sousa

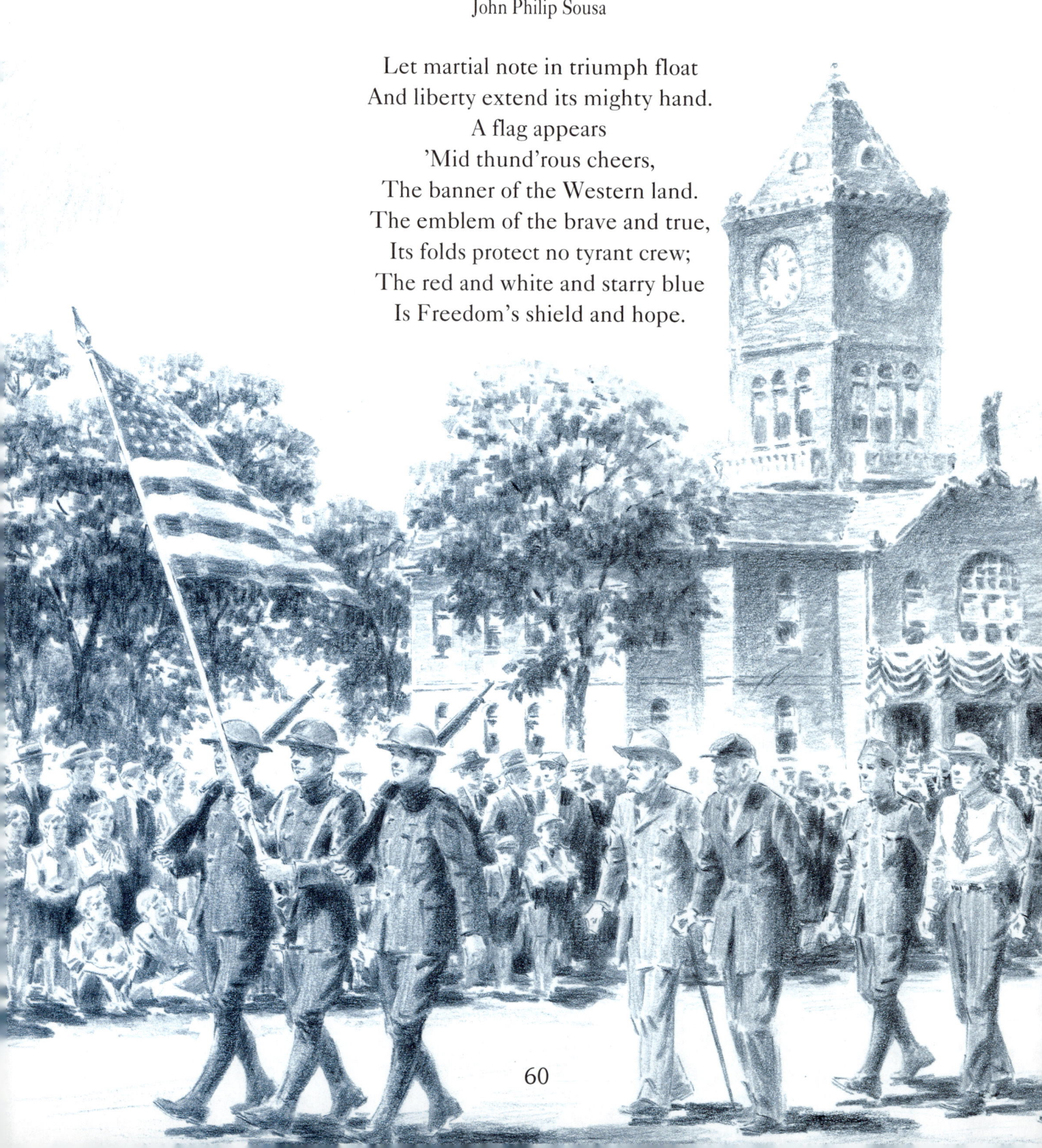

Let martial note in triumph float
And liberty extend its mighty hand.
A flag appears
'Mid thund'rous cheers,
The banner of the Western land.
The emblem of the brave and true,
Its folds protect no tyrant crew;
The red and white and starry blue
Is Freedom's shield and hope.

Let eagle shriek from lofty peak
The neverending watchword of our land.
Let summer breeze
Waft through the trees
The echo of the chorus grand.
Sing out for liberty and light,
Sing out for freedom and the right,
Sing out for Union and its might,
Oh, patriotic sons!

Other nations may deem their flags the best
And cheer them with fervid elation,
But the flag of the North

And South and West
Is the flag of flags, the flag of
Freedom's nation.
Hurrah for the flag of the free,
May it wave as our standard forever.
The gem of the land and the sea,
The Banner of the Right.

Let despots remember the day
When our fathers, with mighty endeavor,
Proclaimed as they marched to the fray,
That by their might and by their right
It waves forever.

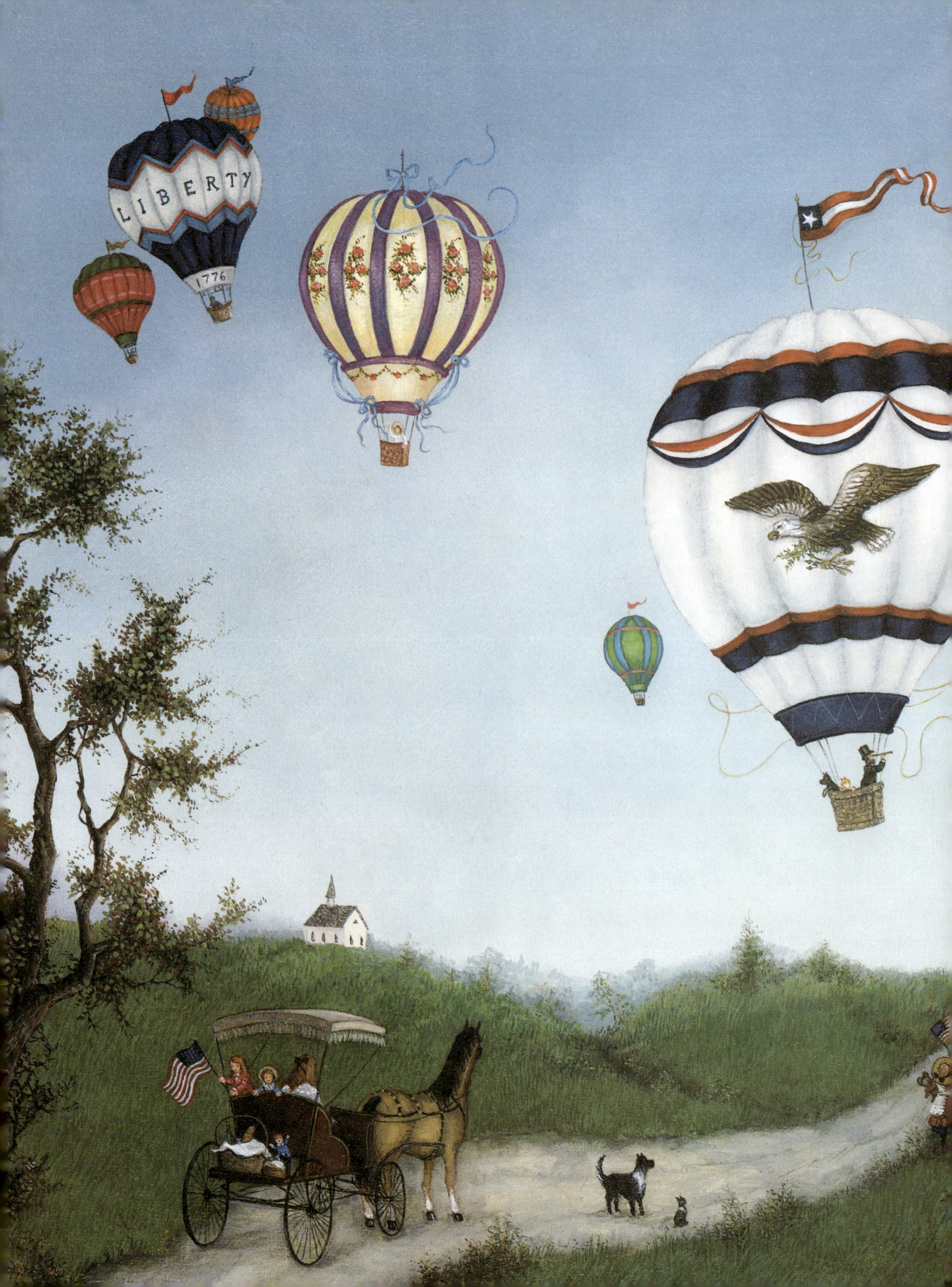
LIBERTY
1776

Wave on, O Flag

Edna Moore Schultz

Wave on, O Flag of this fair land,
Wave high where men of goodwill stand!
Wave over shops and ships at sea,
Wave as a symbol of the free!

Wave on, O Flag with star-splashed square,
Wave out for freedom everywhere!
Wave constantly the red and white
And blue, bold standard for the right!

Wave gently over every grave
Where patriot has died to save
Our country from the tyrant's aim!
Wave in our nation's glorious name!

Wave on from Maine to Washington
In winter's cold and summer's sun.
From mountaintop to restless sea,
Dear Flag, wave on for liberty!

UP, UP AND AWAY
Original painting by Linda Nelson Stocks

BITS & PIECES

We plough the fields and scatter
The good seed on the land,
But it is fed and watered
By God's almighty hand.

    Jane Montgomery Campbell

Before green apples blush,
    Before green nuts embrown,
Why, one day in the country
    Is worth a month in town.

    Christina Rossetti

God made the country and man made the town. What wonder, then, that health and virtue should most abound and least be threatened in the fields and groves.

    William Cowper

Mountains are the beginning and the end of all natural scenery.

    John Ruskin

I consider it the best part of an education
to have been born and brought up in the country.

    Amos Bronson Alcott

How blessed is he who leads a country life,
Unvexed with anxious cares, and void of strife!

    John Dryden

What does he plant who plants a tree?
He plants a friend of sun and sky;
He plants the flag of breezes free,
The shaft of beauty towering high;
He plants a home to heaven anigh
For song and mother-croon of bird
In hushed and happy twilight heard,
The treble of heaven's harmony;
These things he plants who plants a tree.

    Henry Cuyler Bunner

Prairie Memories

Hamlin Garland

O memory, what conjury is thine!
Once more the sun shines on the wheat;
Once more I drink the wind like wine,
When bursts the lark's song wildly sweet
From out the rain-wet, new-mown grass;
I hear the sickle's clattering sweep,
And peals of laughter lightly pass
From lip to lip; again, heap
The odorous windrows rank by rank.
Silent the tumult of the street.
From granite pavement's ceaseless clank,
From grinding hooves and jar of car,
I flee and lave my boyish feet
Where bee-lodged clover blossoms are!

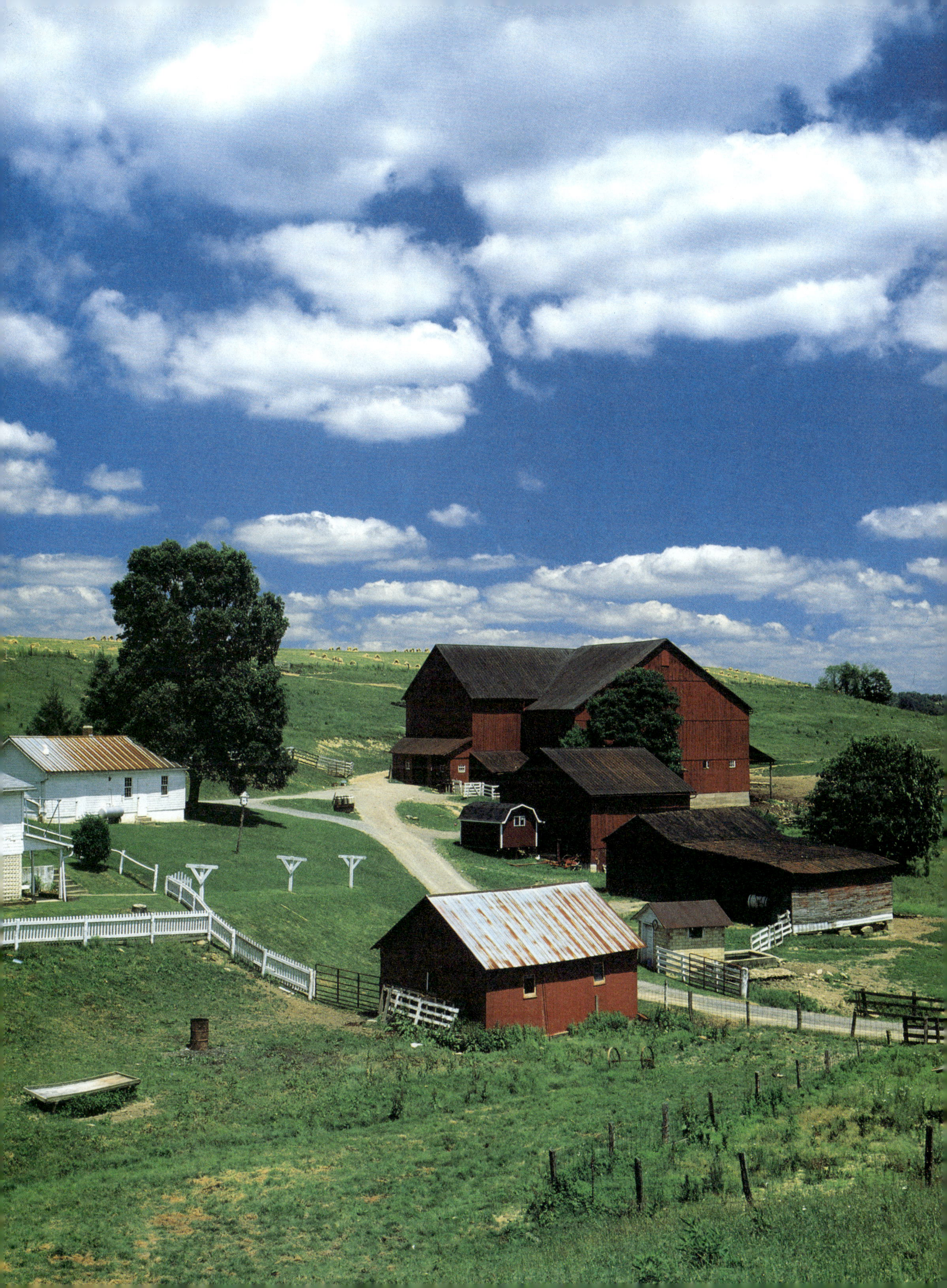

LEGENDARY AMERICANS

Nancy Skarmeas

Willa Cather

In 1883, Virginia farmer Charles Cather uprooted his family and led them across the country to Webster County, Nebraska, where they joined a small group of pioneers from their native state making a new life on the Great Plains. The move was difficult for all the Cathers, particularly for eldest daughter Willa, for whom the Cather family farm had been a paradise. She had freely roamed the familiar woods and fields and basked in the love and care of her closely knit extended family. The vast, strange spaces of the Great Plains and the isolation of pioneer life were a shock to the young girl, and she resisted the change, longing for the comforts of home.

Nevertheless, Nebraska was Cather's new home; and as the days turned into months and years, she developed a bond with her neighbors on the Plains and a respect for the life the frontier demanded. She met families from all across the United States and from places as far away as Sweden and Germany. Like the Cathers, these people had left behind the comforts of home for the challenge of the frontier. They lived in rough sod houses, isolated from family, friends, and neighbors, yet they clung to their basic values and traditions and remained true to their desire to make a good life in the West. These people taught Willa Cather to accept and love frontier life, and, years later, provided the inspiration for her simple and graceful stories about the life of the American pioneer.

Although her years on the Great Plains provided the inspiration for almost the entire body of Willa Cather's fictional work, her time there was, in fact, very short. After graduating from high school in Red Cloud, Nebraska, Cather attended the University of Nebraska. From there, she embarked upon a career in journalism, holding jobs ranging from copy editor at a Pittsburgh, Pennsylvania, newspaper to editor of *McClure's* magazine in New York City. All the while, she nurtured a growing interest in fiction writing. In 1912, despite great success as an editor, Cather resigned her post at *McClure's* and devoted herself full time to fiction.

Willa Cather's body of work was immediately recognized as among the best in American fiction. Her stories celebrated the courage and commitment of the American pioneer and also lamented the passing of the frontier era as the true pioneers were joined by those with no respect for the land and with impure motives for settling it. The novels *O Pioneers!* and *My Antonia* pay tribute to the spirit of the immigrant pioneers who looked to the American West to fulfill their dreams of a better life. Both feature strong female farmers who cherish the challenge and the opportunity of the frontier and who possess the courage and strength to maintain their values in the face of great hardship.

Other works, including *One of Ours*, for which Cather won the Pulitzer Prize, and *A Lost Lady*, lament the passing of the true pioneer era. *A Lost Lady*'s Mrs. Forrester is a pioneer woman in a railroad town who is left behind by the changing times and destined to live out her days longing for a way of life gone forever. Cather also wrote about the great pioneers of history, people like the French missionaries in the American Southwest and the French Canadians in Quebec, who shared the spirit of the families of the Great Plains.

After the age of eighteen, Willa Cather lived far away from Nebraska. Her years were split between New York City in the winters and New England in the summers. She traveled to some of the most prestigious American universities to receive honorary degrees, saw much of Europe, and earned countless awards and prizes for her fiction. When she died in New York City at the age of seventy-five, she was buried, at her own request, not in Nebraska, but in the small town of Jaffrey, New Hampshire, where she had spent part of many autumns writing.

Willa Cather experienced so much of life. She knew the comfort and security of life on a Virginia farm steeped in family history and tradition as well as life among the nation's literary elite in New York City, but nothing in her life touched her as much as her nine years on the Great Plains. No experience had been as challenging or as rewarding, and no experience had taught her more about the human spirit. Throughout her life, Cather spoke of Nebraska with nostalgic longing; yet she never returned to live on the Plains, in part because her talents and dreams had taken her beyond small-town life, and also because she knew that the life she remembered had passed from existence. Instead, Willa Cather chose to preserve her memory of the life she knew on the Great Plains in the pages of her short stories and novels. Her work pays constant tribute to the land and the life that formed her character and gave her the strength and courage to make a life of her own elsewhere.

In her will, Willa Cather asked that her works never be sold to movie makers. Her desire was that her fiction remain as authentic and independent as the life and the people that inspired it. Readers should be thankful for this, for as a result we have not only entertaining and enlightening stories, but also an authentic record of a wonderful, heroic era in American history.

TRAVELER'S Diary

Tim Hamling

Railroad Town's Blacksmith Shop. Photo courtesy of Stuhr Museum of the Prairie Pioneer.

Stuhr Museum of the Prairie Pioneer

As the great railroads linking East to West in the late nineteenth century spread across the fertile plains of Nebraska, small prairie communities developed along the railways' routes. Depending on their proximity to the rail lines, some of these towns prospered while others struggled to survive. Near Grand Island, Nebraska, in the south-central part of the state, one of these prairie communities has been preserved as part of the Stuhr Museum of the Prairie Pioneer to offer a model of pioneer life during the last decades of the 1800s.

The Stuhr Museum's two-hundred-acre complex includes two main exhibit halls housing artifacts from Nebraska's thriving pioneer period, 1860-1910. In the main museum, designed by the renowned architect Edward Durrell Stone, articles of clothing and household furnishings decorate period rooms designed to resemble the early pioneers' homes. A second hall, the Gus Fonner Memorial Rotunda, showcases collections of Native American and Old West memorabilia. The exhibit reveals the contrasting cultures of the Plains Indians and the western pioneers who made their homes in the area.

A short walk from the exhibit halls is Railroad Town, Nebraska, a prairie community recreated from century-old homes and shops restored to their late nineteenth-century condition. The buildings were all moved from other locations to the forty-acre town patterned after those communities built along the Union Pacific rail systems. Horse-drawn carriages carry visitors and costumed "townspeople" along Main Street, where a blacksmith shop, mercantile store, saloon, and other shops recreate the pioneer atmosphere.

A residential area of historic homes lies

70

The shops of Front Street in Railroad Town.
Photo courtesy of Stuhr Museum of the Prairie Pioneer.

tucked behind Railroad Town's busy commercial district. Nineteenth-century furnishings provide a clue to Nebraska's pioneer lifestyle. The most noted home in the area is Henry Fonda's childhood cottage built in Grand Island in 1883. Under Fonda's guidance and financial support, the small house was moved to Railroad Town to become part of the Stuhr Museum.

The railroads that were so instrumental in the development of Nebraska's pioneer settlements are displayed in a railyard bordering Railroad Town. A depot built in 1887 and original steam locomotives from 1901 and 1908 have been preserved to educate visitors on the nation's first great system of transportation.

Since farming provided the livelihood for so many of Nebraska's pioneers, the Stuhr Museum contains an exhibit of antique farm machinery and equipment that includes an 1880 threshing machine and steam tractors. Although these machines are crude by today's standards, they were a blessing to the farmers who were able to cultivate more of Nebraska's fertile prairies than would have otherwise been possible.

Other rural communities representative of Nebraska's nineteenth-century culture have been maintained as part of the museum. A Pawnee Indian Earth Lodge containing authentic clothing, furnishings, tools, and weapons teaches visitors about the Native Americans who shared the land with the pioneers. Nearby, a country church, school, and several farm buildings mark the remnants of the Runnelsburg community. The town's founder hoped the railroads would build to his town; but when they did not, Runnelsburg struggled to survive.

Unlike some of the early prairie communities, the Stuhr Museum has prospered since its founding in 1960 when Grand Island businessman and history enthusiast Leo B. Stuhr donated the first land and money to finance the museum that would bear his name. Stuhr's foresight has preserved an integral part of American culture. Like the railroads that linked East and West, the Stuhr Museum connects today's society with the communities that preceded it.

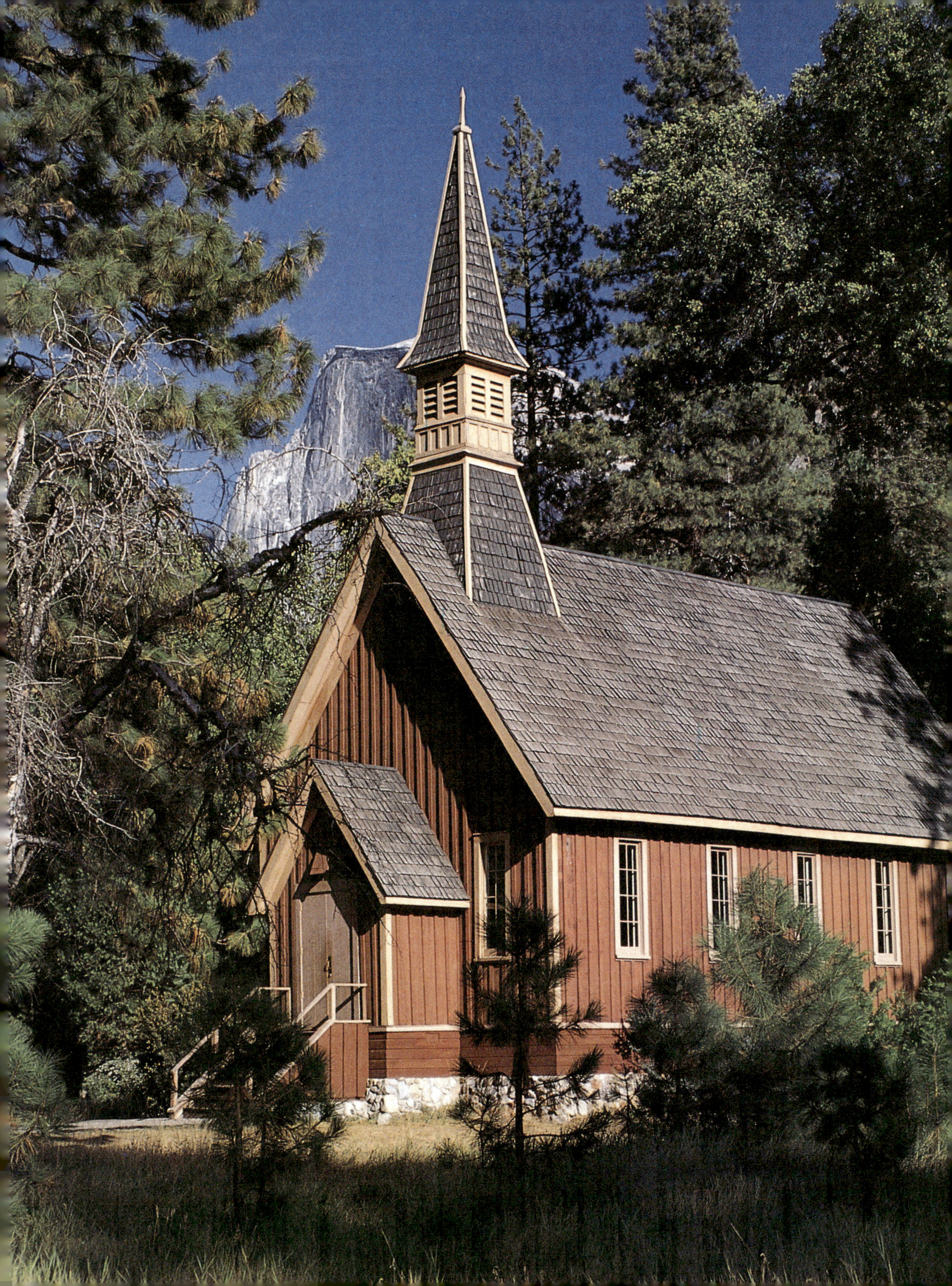

Country Church

Brian F. King

I think the nearest place to God
That men will ever find
Lies sheltered in a country church
With faith and hope enshrined.

A peaceful, weathered country church
With stained-glass windowpanes,
A church that dreams the hours away
In sun and wind and rain.

A church with mossy flagstone paths,
Great oak doors opened wide,
And gentle folk to welcome you
When you set foot inside.

A church where hearts are rich with love
For He Who fills with grace
The hearts of those who help sustain
The Shepherd's meeting place.

Photo Opposite
YOSEMITE CHAPEL
Yosemite National Park, California
Laatsch-Hupp Photography

ROBIN ON LAWN. Adam Jones, Photographer.

Country CHRONICLE
Lansing Christman

For the last several years, robins have selected the ledge of an upstairs bedroom at the home of one of my neighbors as their nesting place. The nest's location gives my neighbors a firsthand view of the sky-blue eggs, the newly hatched young, and finally, the time the fledglings try their wings for their first venture into the world around them. We had the same experience when we lived in a two-story farmhouse. The ledge of a window at the top of a winding stairway frequently served as a housing site. From their nest emanated the sweet notes of the robins' song.

A robin's song is full of hope and inspiration, best described as a "rolling carol that is both cheerful and melodious." The song cheers us at dawn as the day's light begins to "wash away" the glitter of the stars in the sky overhead.

ROBINS AT NEST. Adam Jones, Photographer.

We hear the carols again as the day's sun lowers in the western sky.

I've heard an old adage about robins singing for rain during a period of drought when the sun has baked and parched the land. When the skies at last begin to hint that relief is on the way, the robins' carols become persistent and musical, so full of hope.

Robins are friendly birds; they come to our lawns and nest in our dooryard trees and shrubs and in the lilacs along the wall. Long ago my father wrote about robins nesting in his lilacs:

> Robin of my lilac, who,
> Having such a home as you,
> Would not be a poet too?
> Thus at dawn I hear him sing
> Where the lilac censers swing.

Let the robins come to your yard, to your trees, bushes, and shrubs. Let them claim their nesting sites as near as they choose. Those sky-blue eggs you see will become another generation of carols joining the chorus of birdsong in your neighborhood next year.

The author of two published books, Lansing Christman has been contributing to Ideals for almost twenty years. Mr. Christman has also been published in several American, foreign, and braille anthologies. He lives in rural South Carolina.

God of the Open Air

Henry van Dyke

Thou who hast made thy dwelling fair
With flowers beneath,
Above with starry lights,
And set thine altars everywhere,
On mountain heights,
In woodlands dim with many a dream,
In valleys bright with springs,
And on the curving capes of every stream;

Thou who hast taken to thyself
The wings of morning
To abide upon the secret places of the sea,
And on far islands where the tide
Visits the beauty of untrodden shores,
Waiting for worshippers to come to thee
In thy great out-of-doors!
To thee I turn, to thee I make my prayer,
God of the open air.

Photo Opposite
YOSEMITE FALLS
Yosemite National Park, California
Bob Clemenz Photography

Thanksgiving on a Summer's Day

Peter Marshall

We give Thee thanks, Lord of heaven and earth, for the promise of summer, for the beauty of this day—a day
    that shall ripen grain,
    that shall provide good things for the table,
    that shall make all growing things rejoice,
    that shall make more sweet the music of the
        birds,
    that shall make more beautiful the gardens
        which Thou hast planted and watered.

We thank Thee for the fertility of the land that encourages us to sow and to plant. We thank Thee for the dependence of the seasons, for all Thy sustaining providence by which men work today and harvest tomorrow.

We well know, our Father, that we are not worthy of Thy bounty, but help us to be good stewards of that bounty. We thank Thee for the endless delight of our lives on this lovely earth. Amen.

Announcing a NEW IDEALS Patriotic Edition
Hear America Singing

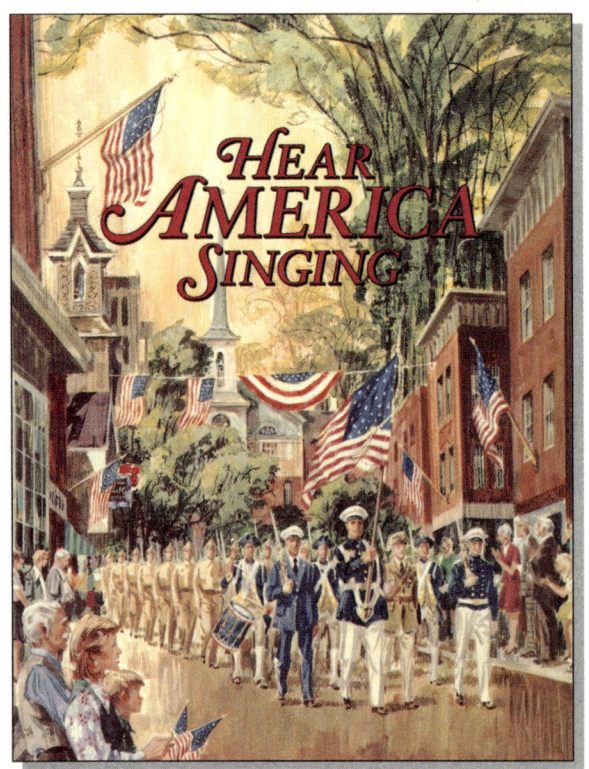

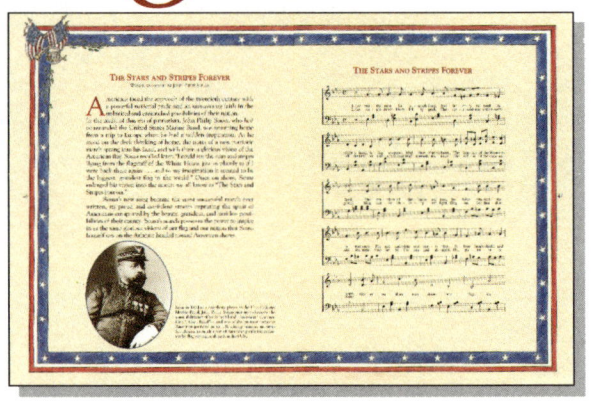

John Philip Sousa, the master of marches, composed "The Stars and Stripes Forever."

"O say can you see, by the dawn's early light; What so proudly we hailed at the twilight's last gleaming." Is there an American alive whose heart does not skip a beat as this anthem begins and the majestic words tell again the story of that "perilous night" which marked the birth of a sovereign nation?

Ideals is pleased to announce the publication of a brand-new 80-page book with heavy paper cover and featuring twenty of these stirring patriotic songs. Our national anthem is only one of this patriotic repertoire giving thanks for our freedoms, proclaiming pride in our heritage, and calling a nation to war. These stirring patriotic songs signify what it means to be an American, and every *Ideals* home will want to own this beautiful new publication.

Luxurious Illustrations
Each title features the score and story behind its composition and is magnificently illustrated with color photography, well-known paintings, or patriotic artwork which only enhances the meaning of the songs.

20 Favorite Patriotic Songs
Some of the songs and their stories included are:
- ☆ "America" and "America the Beautiful"
- ☆ "The Battle Hymn of the Republic"
- ☆ "The Star Spangled Banner" and "Yankee Doodle"
- ☆ "The Stars and Stripes Forever"
- ☆ "The Marine's Hymn" and "Semper Paratus"
- ☆ "When Johnny Comes Marching Home Again"

Stay-Open Binding
A special "stay-open" binding makes this beautiful book perfectly at home on the piano, coffee table, or bookshelf. And the whole family will treasure this beautiful volume for a long time to come.

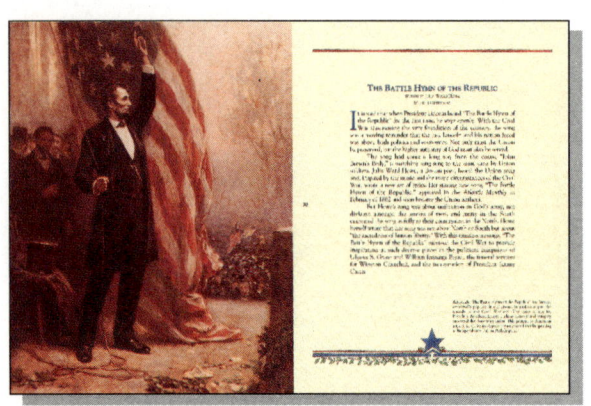

A painting of President Lincoln illustrates the story behind "The Battle Hymn of the Republic."

Supply Is Limited. Order Today!
Single issue only $7.95 plus $3.00 postage and handling.
(Order #11172A)

Special Offer: 5 copies with envelopes for gift presentation only $34.95 plus $3.50 postage and handling.
(Order #07778A)

Fill out the order form; make checks payable to Ideals Publishing Corp., and enclose in envelope provided.
Or send orders to:
Ideals Publishing Corporation
Dept.: Hear America Singing
P.O. Box 148000
Nashville, TN 37214-8000
Or call toll-free 1-800-558-4343